W9-BRB-243

SUPER SIMPLE

BAR

cookies

EASY COOKIE RECIPES FOR KIDS!

ALEX KUSKOWSKI

Consulting Editor, Diane Craig, M.A./Reading Specialist

Super Sandcastle

An Imprint of Abdo Publishing
abdopublishing.com

abdopublishing.com

Published by Abdo Publishing, a division of ABDO, PO Box 398166, Minneapolis, Minnesota 55439. Copyright © 2016 by Abdo Consulting Group, Inc. International copyrights reserved in all countries. No part of this book may be reproduced in any form without written permission from the publisher. Super SandCastle™ is a trademark and logo of Abdo Publishing.

Printed in the United States of America, North Mankato, Minnesota
102015
012016

THIS BOOK CONTAINS RECYCLED MATERIALS

Editor: Liz Salzmann
Content Developer: Nancy Tuminelly
Cover and Interior Design and Production: Mighty Media, Inc.
Photo Credits: Mighty Media, Inc., Shutterstock

The following manufacturers/names appearing in this book are trademarks: Calumet®, PAM®, C&H®, Nutella®, Karo®, Land O Lakes®, Market Pantry™, Proctor Silex®

Library of Congress Cataloging-in-Publication Data
Kuskowski, Alex, author.
  Super simple bar cookies : easy cookie recipes for kids! / Alex Kuskowski.
    pages cm. -- (Super simple cookies)
  ISBN 978-1-62403-946-1
  1. Bars (Desserts)--Juvenile literature. 2. Cookies--Juvenile literature. 3. Baking--Juvenile literature. I. Title.
  TX772.K774 2016
  641.86'54--dc23
                    2015020591

Super SandCastle™ books are created by a team of professional educators, reading specialists, and content developers around five essential components—phonemic awareness, phonics, vocabulary, text comprehension, and fluency—to assist young readers as they develop reading skills and strategies and increase their general knowledge. All books are written, reviewed, and leveled for guided reading and early reading intervention programs for use in shared, guided, and independent reading and writing activities to support a balanced approach to literacy instruction.

TO ADULT HELPERS

Help your child learn to cook! Cooking lets children practice math and science. It teaches kids about responsibility and boosts their confidence. Plus they get to make some great food!

Before getting started, set ground rules for using the kitchen, cooking tools, and ingredients. There should always be adult supervision when use of a sharp tool, oven, or stove is required. Be aware of the symbols below that indicate when special care is necessary.

So, put on your apron and get ready to cheer on your new chef!

SYMBOLS

Hot!
This recipe requires the use of a stove or oven. You will need adult supervision and assistance.

Sharp!
This recipe includes the use of a sharp utensil such as a knife or grater. Ask an adult to help out.

Nuts!
This recipe includes nuts. Find out whether anyone you are serving has a nut allergy.

CONTENTS

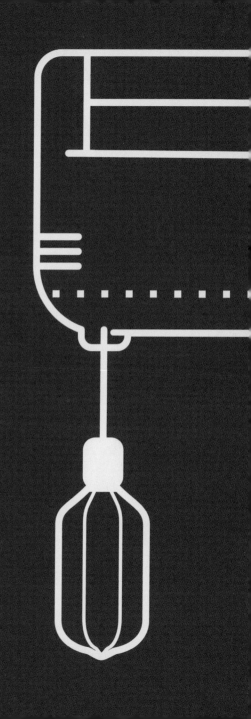

SET THE BAR HIGH!

Get ready to make a whole new kind of cookie! Start baking bar cookies. They are fun to make. It is easy to take them wherever you go. They are a fun snack to make anytime.

The bar **recipes** in this book are super simple. Cooking teaches you about food, measuring, and following directions. And you get to have **delicious** cookies! Share your tasty creations with family and friends.

COOKING BASICS

Think Safety!

- Ask an adult to help you use a knife. Place things on a cutting board to cut them.

- Clean up spills right away.

- Keep things away from the edge of the table or **counter**.

- Ask an adult to help you use the oven.

- Ask for help if you cannot reach something.

Using the Oven

- Preheat the oven while making the **recipe**.

- Use oven-safe dishes.

- Use pot holders or oven mitts to hold hot things.

- Do not touch the oven door. It can be very hot.

- Set a timer. Check the food and bake longer if needed.

Before Baking

- Get **permission** from an adult.

- Wash your hands.

- Read the recipe at least once.

- Set out the ingredients and tools you will need.

- Keep a **towel** close by for cleaning up spills.

When You're Done

- Let the cookies cool completely.

- Store the cookies in **containers**. Put a sheet of waxed paper in between the **layers** of cookies.

- Put all the ingredients and tools away.

- Wash all the dishes and **utensils**. Clean up your work space.

MEASURING INGREDIENTS

Wet Ingredients

Set a measuring cup on the **counter**. Add the liquid. Stop when it reaches the amount you need. Check the measurement from eye level.

Dry Ingredients

Dip the measuring cup or spoon into the dry ingredient. Fill it with a little more than you need. Use the back of a dinner knife to remove the extra.

Moist Ingredients

Measure ingredients such as brown sugar and dried fruit differently. Press them down into the measuring cup.

DID YOU KNOW THIS = THAT?

There are different ways to measure the same amount.

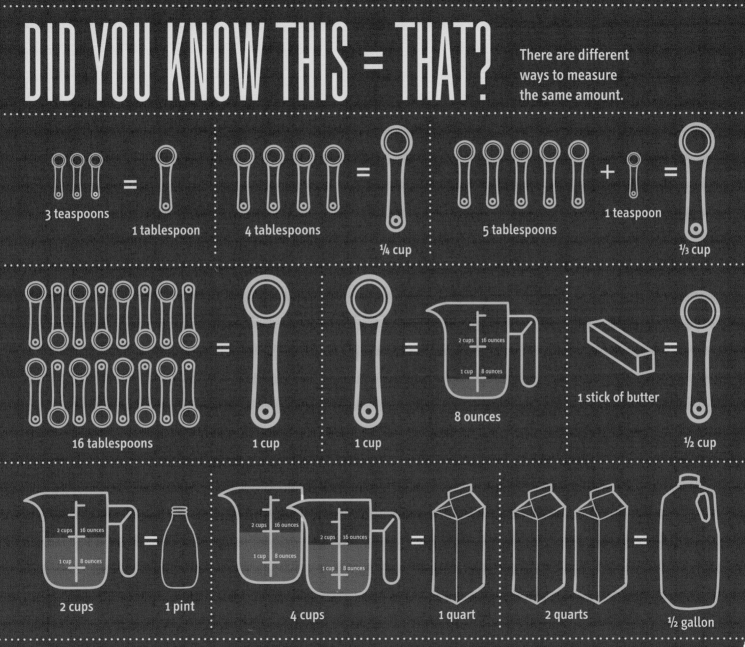

3 teaspoons = 1 tablespoon

4 tablespoons = ¼ cup

5 tablespoons + 1 teaspoon = ⅓ cup

16 tablespoons = 1 cup

1 cup = 8 ounces

1 stick of butter = ½ cup

2 cups = 1 pint

4 cups = 1 quart

2 quarts = ½ gallon

COOKING TERMS

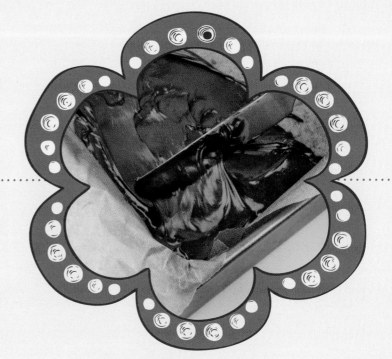

DRIZZLE

Drizzle means to slowly pour a liquid over something.

SPREAD

Spread means to make a smooth **layer** with a spoon, knife, or rubber spatula.

WHISK

Whisk means to beat quickly
by hand with a whisk or a fork.

ZEST

Zest means to scrape the peel from
a fruit with a zester or grater.

KITCHEN UTENSILS

spoon

sharp knife

measuring spoons

measuring cups

candy thermometer

medium saucepan

cutting board

electric mixer

whisk

rubber spatula

mixing spoon

grater

microwave-safe mixing bowl

baking pans

baking sheet

mixing bowls

pot holders

parchment paper

13

INGREDIENTS

all-purpose flour

baking powder

brown sugar

butter

butterscotch chips

canola oil

chocolate spread

corn syrup

crispy rice cereal

eggs

flaked coconut

graham crackers

heavy cream

lemons

miniature marshmallows

non-stick cooking spray

peanuts

peanut butter chips

pecans

powdered sugar

salt

sea salt

semi-sweet chocolate chips

sweetened condensed milk

unsweetened cocoa powder

vanilla extract

white sugar

15

sweet brownie bites

MAKES 16 BARS

INGREDIENTS

non-stick cooking spray
½ cup butter
1 cup white sugar
2 eggs
1 teaspoon vanilla extract
6 tablespoons unsweetened
  cocoa powder
½ cup all-purpose flour
¼ teaspoon salt
¼ teaspoon baking
  powder
½ cup semi-sweet
  chocolate chips
½ cup powdered sugar

TOOLS

8 × 8-inch baking dish
microwave-safe mixing bowl
mixing spoon
measuring cups
measuring spoons
rubber spatula
pot holders

1 Preheat the oven to 350 degrees.
   Grease the baking dish with
   non-stick cooking spray.

2 Put the butter in a microwave-safe
   bowl. Microwave it for 30 seconds.
   Stir in the sugar, eggs, and vanilla.

3 Add the cocoa powder, flour, salt, and
   baking powder. Mix well. Stir in the
   chocolate chips.

4 Pour the batter into the baking dish.
   Smooth it with a spatula.

5 Bake for 25 minutes. Take the baking
   dish out of the oven. Sprinkle the
   powdered sugar over the brownies.
   Let them cool.

lucky
lemon
bars

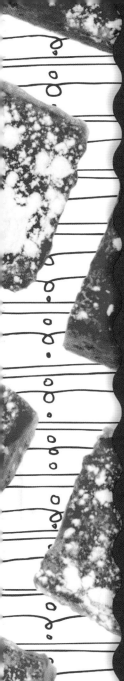

INGREDIENTS

1 cup butter
2¼ cups all-purpose flour
2 cups white sugar
¼ teaspoon salt
3 lemons
4 eggs

TOOLS

8 × 11-inch baking pan
parchment paper
mixing bowls
measuring cups
measuring spoons
electric mixer
grater
sharp knife
cutting board
whisk
pot holders

1   Preheat the oven to 350 degrees. Cover the pan with parchment paper.

2   Put the butter, 2 cups flour, ½ cup sugar, and salt in a medium bowl. Mix with an electric mixer.

3   Press the mixture evenly into the bottom of the pan. Bake for 15 minutes. Take it out and let it cool.

4   Zest one lemon. Cut the lemons in half. Squeeze the juice into a small bowl. Add the zest to the juice. Add 1½ cups sugar, ¼ cup flour, and eggs. Whisk the ingredients together.

5   Pour the lemon mixture over the crust. Bake for 24 minutes. Chill the pan in the refrigerator for 2 hours.

crispy rice bars

MAKES 16 BARS

INGReDIenTS

non-stick cooking spray
3 tablespoons butter
1½ teaspoons vanilla
   extract
4 cups miniature
   marshmallows
5 cups crispy rice cereal

. . . .

TOOLS

8 × 8-inch baking pan
medium saucepan
measuring cups
measuring spoons
mixing spoon
pot holders
rubber spatula

1 **Grease** the baking pan with non-stick cooking spray.

2 Melt the butter in a medium saucepan over low heat.

3 Add the vanilla and marshmallows. Stir until the marshmallows melt. Take the pan off of the heat.

4 Add the cereal to the saucepan. Stir until the cereal is coated with the marshmallow mixture.

5 Press the mixture evenly in the baking pan. Let it cool for 2 hours.

21

seventh heaven bars

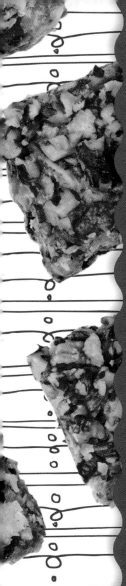

Ingredients

1 package graham crackers

½ cup butter, melted

1 14-ounce can sweetened condensed milk

1 cup butterscotch chips

1 cup semi-sweet chocolate chips

1⅓ cups flaked coconut

1 cup chopped pecans

Tools

9 × 13-inch baking pan

parchment paper

plastic zipper bag

rolling pin

measuring cups

mixing bowl

rubber spatula

measuring spoons

pot holders

1 Preheat the oven to 350 degrees. Cover the baking pan with parchment paper.

2 Put some graham crackers in a plastic bag. Use a rolling pin to crush the crackers. Put the **crumbs** in a measuring cup. Repeat until you have 1½ cup of crumbs.

3 Put the graham cracker crumbs and butter in a medium bowl. Stir well. Press the mixture evenly into the bottom of the pan.

4 Pour the condensed milk evenly over the crumb mixture.

5 Sprinkle each of the remaining ingredients, in order, over the pan.

6 Bake 25 minutes or until light brown. Take the pan out of the oven. Let it cool.

chewy
peanut
bites

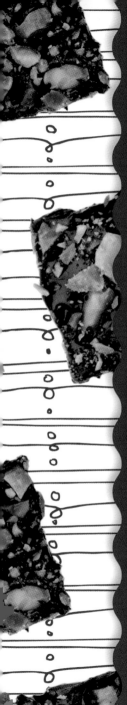

MAKES 24 BARS

INGREDIENTS

1 cup butter
1 cup brown sugar
1 teaspoon vanilla extract
1 egg
2 cups all-purpose flour
¼ teaspoon salt
1 cup chocolate spread
½ cup chopped peanuts

. . . .

TOOLS

9 × 13-inch baking pan
parchment paper
mixing bowl
measuring cups
measuring spoons
electric mixer
rubber spatula
pot holders
dinner knife

1. Preheat the oven to 350 degrees. Cover the baking pan with parchment paper.

2. Put the butter, brown sugar, vanilla, and egg in a large bowl. Mix with an electric mixer. Mix in the flour and salt.

3. Press the mixture evenly into the baking pan. Bake for 25 minutes. Take the pan out of the oven. Let it cool for 30 minutes.

4. Spread the chocolate spread over the crust. Sprinkle the nuts on top.

sweet caramel pieces

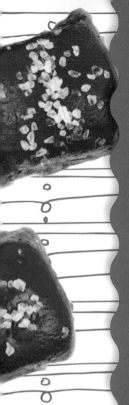

INGREDIENTS

2 cups butter

1½ cups brown sugar

¾ cup powdered sugar

½ teaspoon salt

2 cups all-purpose flour

5 teaspoons vanilla extract

3 teaspoons sea salt

¾ cup corn syrup

4 tablespoons white sugar

4 tablespoons heavy cream

TOOLS

9 × 13-inch baking pan

parchment paper

mixing bowls

measuring cups

measuring spoons

electric mixer

pot holders

medium saucepan

mixing spoon

candy thermometer

spoon

1 Preheat the oven to 325 degrees. Cover the baking pan with parchment paper.

2 Put 1 cup butter, ½ cup brown sugar, and the powdered sugar in a large bowl. Beat with an electric mixer.

3 Mix in the salt, flour, and 3 teaspoons vanilla.

4 Spread the mixture evenly in the bottom of the pan.

5 Bake for 25 minutes or until the crust is light brown. Let it cool.

6 Put 1 cup butter, 1 cup brown sugar, 1 teaspoon sea salt, and the corn syrup, white sugar, and cream in a saucepan.

7 Bring the mixture to a boil over high heat.

8 Put the candy thermometer in the pan. Cook the mixture 5 to 10 minutes until candy thermometer reads 248 degrees. Take the pan off the heat.

9 Stir in 2 teaspoons vanilla.

10 Pour the mixture onto the crust. Refrigerate the pan for 4 hours.

11 Sprinkle 2 teaspoons of sea salt over the **caramel**.

nutty chocolate slices

MAKES 24 BARS

INGREDIENTS

1 14-ounce jar lightly salted peanuts

2 cups peanut butter chips

1 14-ounce can sweetened condensed milk

3 tablespoons butter

2 cups miniature marshmallows

2 cups semi-sweet chocolate chips

2 tablespoons canola oil

· · · · · · · · · · · · · · · ·

TOOLS

9 × 13-inch baking pan

baking sheet

parchment paper

rubber spatula

measuring cups

measuring spoons

microwave-safe mixing bowl

pot holders

1 Cover the baking pan and baking sheet with parchment paper. Spread half the peanuts evenly in the baking pan.

2 Put the peanut butter chips, condensed milk, and butter in a microwave-safe bowl. Microwave on high for 30 seconds. Take it out and stir the mixture. Repeat heating and stirring until the ingredients are melted. Stir in the marshmallows.

3 Spread the mixture evenly over the peanuts in the baking pan.

4 Sprinkle the other half of the peanuts over the top. Press the mixture flat with a rubber spatula. Refrigerate for 2 hours.

5 Put the chocolate chips and canola oil in a microwave-safe bowl. Microwave for 30 seconds. Take it out and stir the melted chips. Drizzle the melted chocolate over the bars. Refrigerate for 1 hour.

GLOSSARY

caramel – a chewy candy made from milk, butter, and burned sugar.

container – something that other things can be put into.

counter – a level surface where food is made.

delicious – very pleasing to taste or smell.

grease – to coat something with butter, oil, or cooking spray.

layer – one thickness of something that may be over or under another thickness.

permission – when a person in charge says it is okay to do something.

recipe – instructions for making something.

towel – a cloth or paper used for cleaning or drying.

utensil – a tool used to prepare or eat food.